Create the Funeral you want for Le$$

A step-by-step consumer guide and workbook on confidently buying funeral, cemetery and cremation services on a budget

The author of this book is not responsible for the accuracy, durability, suitability or availability of products or services purchased in person, over the internet or through local ads.

Table of Contents

Americans and Death

Death in early America was a normal part of life. It was handled entirely at home. The family laid out the body, usually in the main room. Friends and acquaintances offered support, food and remembrance of better times.

The family or a local carpenter built the coffin. If a coffin was too expensive, a shroud made of family linens was used to wrap the body for burial. The body was buried on the family's land or in a community graveyard. In winter, if the ground was too frozen to dig the grave, the body was kept cool in the root cellar until a grave could be dug in the spring.

Funerals were simple. People died at home or nearby and were quickly buried. People who traveled were often buried where they died. Life moved on.

There was shift in thinking during the Civil War. Advances in communications and transportation made it theoretically possible to return fallen soldiers to their homes so they could be buried with family in a timely manner. But the army faced a challenge; they had to either shorten the time it took to transport the men home or they had to extend the time bodies could be kept in good enough condition to make the trip.

A new sideline sprang up: embalming. Early techniques were tested as soldiers died in the field, with both good and bad results. Abraham Lincoln's embalmed body was carried for two weeks on a funeral train for viewing by people rich and poor, having been embalmed with zinc oxide.

The purpose of embalming then, as it is today, was to preserve the body long enough for family and friends to gather to say goodbye. Embalming was not expected to keep bodies presentable for more than a few days to a few weeks, and that's still true today, although you may hear otherwise from funeral salespeople.

The funeral industry was born.

Funeral "homes" offered an alternative to keeping bodies at the family home before burial.

Coffin manufacturers sprang up to fill the demand for "caskets" (the boxy 4-sided containers you see at funerals today). The old 6-sided "toe pincher coffins" went out of style.

Upgraded wagons became the preferred method of transport.

New cemeteries were established. Ornate headstones marked graves of the well-to-do.

Upper class families looked to funeral homes for burial services and products. Some of those funerals were lavish spectacles that became social events for everyone.

Meanwhile, working class families continued to handle death and burial at home. Embalmers did their work in the family home, tool case in hand.

Another major shift, as powerful as the shift to embalming during the Civil War, produced profound industry changes in the middle years of the 20th century; middle class and lower class families were targeted by the industry as potential customers. Manufacturers and funeral providers expanded their product lines so less fortunate families could afford to "send their relatives off in style." Caskets were marketed as status symbols and the traditional pine box was pushed aside for more expensive woods with heavier ornamentation.

Horse-drawn wagons were replaced by glass-sided coaches, then motorized hearses.

Death became an event across all economic groups. Funeral industry salespeople put pressure on families to show how much they cared by pouring money into the funeral and burial.

Funeral homes became stylized places of reverent extravagance.

Today, the funeral industry markets funerals as "life celebrations" complete with videos, a reception and sometimes even a prerecorded message from the person who died.

Funerals Today

Americans today don't want to talk about death, much less make arrangements for a funeral or cremation. But death comes for all of us, and final disposition follows.

Death forces us to confront our feelings about our relationship with the person who died, what *could* have, what *should* have, what *would* have been if the situation had been different or if there was just a little more time. In the midst of this soul searching, we find ourselves making financial decisions we are largely unprepared to make, decisions that leave too many hard-working people in debt for years.

A full funeral and burial is the third-largest expense most Americans have in life, behind buying a house and buying a car. Most people will only be responsible for a single funeral over their lifetime. Our national squeamishness about death leaves most of us without a clue about how to put together a funeral or cremation and how much it should cost.

The average funeral and burial in America now costs more than $10,000, not because we set out to spend more than we can afford, but because we follow guidance given by death industry professionals who recommend more services than we need.

Most of us go to the nearest funeral home or go to the funeral home the family has used over time and look to the professionals at these businesses to guide us through the process. We follow vague recommended "traditions" or face pressure to "celebrate the life" of the person who died with costly videos, receptions, catering, gravesites with views and oversized headstones.

Let me be clear: I didn't write this guide or create **www.usfuneralcosts.com** to bash the industry as a whole. Many modern death industry professionals are caring, insightful and kind. They're sensitive to budget requirements and they want to help us say goodbye in a way we can afford. There are, however, providers who treat everyone who comes to their establishment as an opportunity to up-sell. They count on customers *not to know* what choices are available, *not to understand* what the law says and *not to expect* affordable pricing.

Large corporations have gobbled up entire groups of family-owned funeral homes over the past fifteen years. Those homes still appear to be locally-owned and community focused, but behind the scenes salespeople compete fiercely with one another for commissions and bonuses based on how much they contribute to the bottom line.

In my hundreds of visits to locally-owned and corporate-owned funeral homes, I found that corporate facilities are likely to start their sales pitch with a pre-bundled "package" that costs $11,000 to $15,000 for the funeral alone. They call it “complete” but the casket and cemetery are not included in that price.

They say that buying each funeral product or service from their ala carte price list can lead to paying more than their “package” pricing. But my research using their price sheets to compare prices shows substantial savings if you know what you want... and if you buy only those items.

You need to be prepared before you shop if you want to save money and stay out of debt. It’s perfectly possible to have a meaningful farewell, but you need to know how.

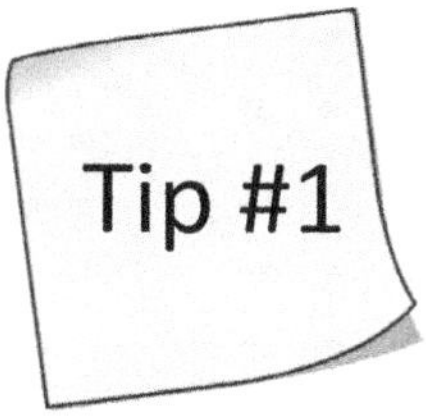

Use this book to spend less time at funeral homes and cemeteries and to get what you want for less.

Let’s start with some budgeting numbers.

Funeral expenses – cemetery costs not included

LIKELY AFFORDABLE AT THIS BUDGET:	$2,000	$4,000	$6,000	$8,000	$10,000	$12,000
pick-up of remains	●	●	●	●	●	●
refigeration of remains	●	●	●	●	●	●
embalming and prep		●	●	●	●	●
casket:						
"alternate" under $1,000	●	●				
$1,000 - 2,000		●	●			
2,000 - 4,000				●	●	
4,000 - 6,000					●	●
death certificate	●	●	●	●	●	●
obituary				●	●	●
service programs and sign-in book					●	●
visitation (open or closed casket)			●	●	●	●
memorial service (body not present)		●	●			
funeral service (body present)			●	●	●	●
gravesite commitment service			●	●	●	●
full gravesite funeral service only		●	●			
cemetery burial with no service	●					
hearse	●	●	●	●	●	●
service vehicle	●	●	●	●	●	●
memorial video			●	●	●	●
reception cookies, desserts				●	●	
catered meal						●
alcohol served					●	●

Cremation Expenses – Urn or other container not included

LIKELY AFFORDABLE AT THIS BUDGET:	$2,000	$4,000	$6,000	$8,000	$10,000	$12,000
cremation:						
"direct" cremation only	●	●				
cremation with simple service	○	●	○			
cremation plus memorial service		●	●	●		
full services				○	●	●
casket plus full services						●
embalming (not recommended)		○	●	●	●	●
refrigeration for non-embalmed	●	●	●	●	●	●
brief family viewing - unembalmed		●	●	●	●	●
rental casket up to $1,500		●	●	●	●	●
wood casket $4,000 and up					●	●

What's your budget? What are the items you absolutely must have for a meaningful service?

When Death Occurs

There are 5 deaths per minute, 296 deaths per hour and 7,115 deaths every day in the U.S.

Although 75% of Americans say they want to die at home, the opposite is true -- 75% of Americans die in medical facilities, often unexpectedly after a heart attack, an accident (a category that includes car crashes, falls and drug overdoses), lung disease or a stroke.

Here are the top ten causes of death in the U.S.:

1. Heart disease
2. Cancer
3. Accidents (unintentional injuries)
4. Chronic lower respiratory diseases
5. Stroke (cerebrovascular diseases)
6. Alzheimer's disease
7. Diabetes
8. Influenza and Pneumonia
9. Kidney problems
10. Intentional self-harm (suicide)

Not one of these deaths is as important as the one you're experiencing. Nor as confusing.

While the experience is different in every case, there are basic processes set in place for survivors to follow after death. Many of those rules depend upon where the death occurred.

In medical facilities it's often the language around illness and death that keeps loved ones from recognizing its approach. Staff use complicated words and terms as if to shield family from the truth. After death, medical staff move on to the next case and the family is tasked with getting the body removed quickly to make room for others in need.

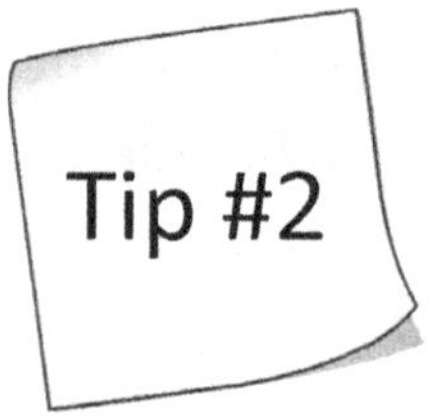

Some hospitals may demand that you have the body removed in two hours or less. Ask them to move the body to their morgue if you're not ready to get started.

If the person dies ***under home hospice care*** the hospice team comes to the house, removes any unused medications and small equipment and makes sure someone in the house can step up and be the leader for what comes next. Surprisingly, many hospice families don't have a plan for after-death care. They're so focused on getting through the strain of facing death that they don't look at what will need to be done after death occurs. Trust me, it happens. It happened to me, and I'm pretty knowledgeable on this stuff.

For families whose loved ones ***die at home unexpectedly***, first responders decide whether there's a reason to think the death is from natural causes or if it is "suspicious." If the death is not suspicious the family must have the body removed by a funeral service provider unless they want to hold the funeral at home (which is completely legal in most states).

> *Note that in some areas, everyone who dies anywhere other than under medical care must be physically examined by a state or county official*

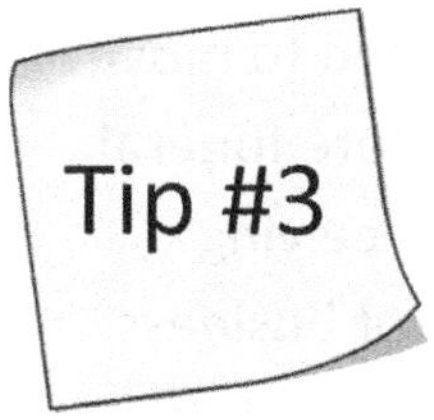

The law in most cases does not require the body be moved from a home in less than 24 hours after death. You have time to think this through.

Whether the death is at a medical facility, in hospice care or at home, emotionally drained family and friends find themselves searching for a funeral home or other provider to remove the body from the place of death even as the weight of their loss begins to settle in.

At a hospital or nursing home a social worker or other staff member may mention a nearby funeral services provider. At home, a first responder may know of a provider they think "does a good job." Be aware that funeral homes in competitive areas may pay for the recommendation.

Tip #4

In competitive areas there may be as many as three times the number of funeral homes as are needed. In those areas every referral is crucial to the bottom line.

Most families assume they can use any funeral home to remove the body and they can change to another provider later without significant cost. Not true. If you need to move the body from one funeral home to another before funeral services the “sending” funeral home and the “receiving” funeral provider will both be paid for their loss of business. They charge between $1,000 and $3,500 on each end, plus airfare/transportation.

Moving the body from one funeral home to another can cost as much as the funeral itself. I can tell you it happens because it happened to my family. The trip my mother made from a Tampa funeral home to a Detroit funeral home after her death cost $7,000, $3,500 for each funeral home. None of us were paying attention in the midst of everything that needed to be done. We didn’t see a final bill until services were complete.

If you need to have a body moved across the city or across the country contact the receiving funeral home and have them make the arrangements. It can cost less.

Which providers would you consider using?
Why?

The Basics of Arranging a Funeral

This guide assumes that you will work with a funeral or cremation provider and have the services provided in a location other than your home. It's legal in all states to have a funeral at home (nine states require a funeral director no matter what you choose to do) but it's not something most families are ready to conquer without real consideration, even though families who do have a home funeral say they find deeper closure and that children are more accepting of death and loss afterwards. I'll talk about home funeral and other newer options near the end of this book.

Here's a quick list of what needs to be done in the few days before death and then through burial. Each of these topics will be covered in depth later in the book.

1. Your direct contact at the funeral home will be called a **funeral director**. This man or woman has attended funeral sciences college as required by your state and has been trained in embalming, business operations, and marketing. Assign one person from among your family and friends to be responsible for making final

decisions if the dying person has not named someone. In most states this falls to the current spouse first, then, if they're unable or unwilling, to surviving children but anyone can do it if agreed upon by survivors.

2. If the dying person has funds to pay for their final expenses **prepare financially** by adding someone to key individual bank accounts so expenses can be paid (all unshared bank accounts and safety deposit boxes will be "locked" until the will is approved, which can take up to a year). If there's not enough time to access bank accounts, surviving loved ones will have to pay out of pocket for services and wait for reimbursement from the estate later. Adding someone to accounts or a safety deposit boxes can only be done while the loved one is still living.

3. Decide what **the budget** is. The average funeral and burial in the U.S. is over ten thousand dollars. Payment is immediately due by check, cash, credit card or insurance. If you have just a fraction of that to spend know your limits and hold firm. This guide will offer lots of suggestions for lovely and meaningful ways you can spend less money while providing the services you want – and can afford -- no matter what your budget is.

4. Decide if the body will be **embalmed**. Embalming replaces body fluids with chemicals that help to preserve the body until burial. Embalming is not legally required but some funeral homes refuse to provide an open-casket funeral when embalming is refused. This refusal is their way of pressuring you to embalm your loved one.

5. **Visit a few funeral homes** and select one to work with. The provider you select will "take the body into their care" when death occurs.

6. Make **funeral plans before death** to save more money. You can save 5% or more on list prices and make more clear-headed decisions when you're not in "immediate need". Keep in mind that saving 5% off an outrageously expensive funeral and burial with a corporate provider is still too expensive for most of us.

7. The funeral provider sets up an "**arrangements consultation**" with key family and friends within hours after the body has been removed from the location of death. The funeral director expects that all choices will be made, prices for all services will be agreed upon and payment will be arranged by cash, credit, check or insurance policy at this meeting. Important note: many funeral homes do not accept insurance policies that have been in

effect for less than 2 years.

8. If no **cemetery arrangements** have been made family members need to shop now. Most cemeteries require a vault, opening and closing, and a headstone for burial, which can add up to more than the gravesite itself. More on cemeteries later.

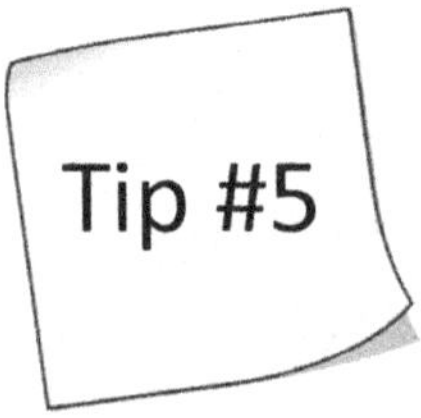

The funeral director may suggest several people come to the arrangements meeting but often that leads to family squabbles.. and higher costs. Only clear-headed people should go.

9. Once arrangements are settled the funeral provider contacts the cemetery on the family's behalf to arrange the day and time for interment (placing the body in the ground or mausoleum).

10. The funeral director orders **death certificates** and prepares other paperwork based on information you report to them. You'll need the birth certificate of the person who died and information about their parents, their last job and employer, survivors' names and other details to fill in the death certificate.

11. A family member brings **a recent clear photo** of their loved one and a burial outfit to the funeral provider. The photo will be used by a cosmetologist to restore the body's features for viewing, but in many cases the family can work with the funeral provider to wash the body a final time and dress them in a favorite outfit, and the family can have their personal hairdresser style the hair a final time.

So now that you've seen the quick list, let's get to the details.

What outfit would you choose for burial? A tennis uniform or a formal gown are equally good choices. This is all about what you want, not what the funeral provider thinks is proper.

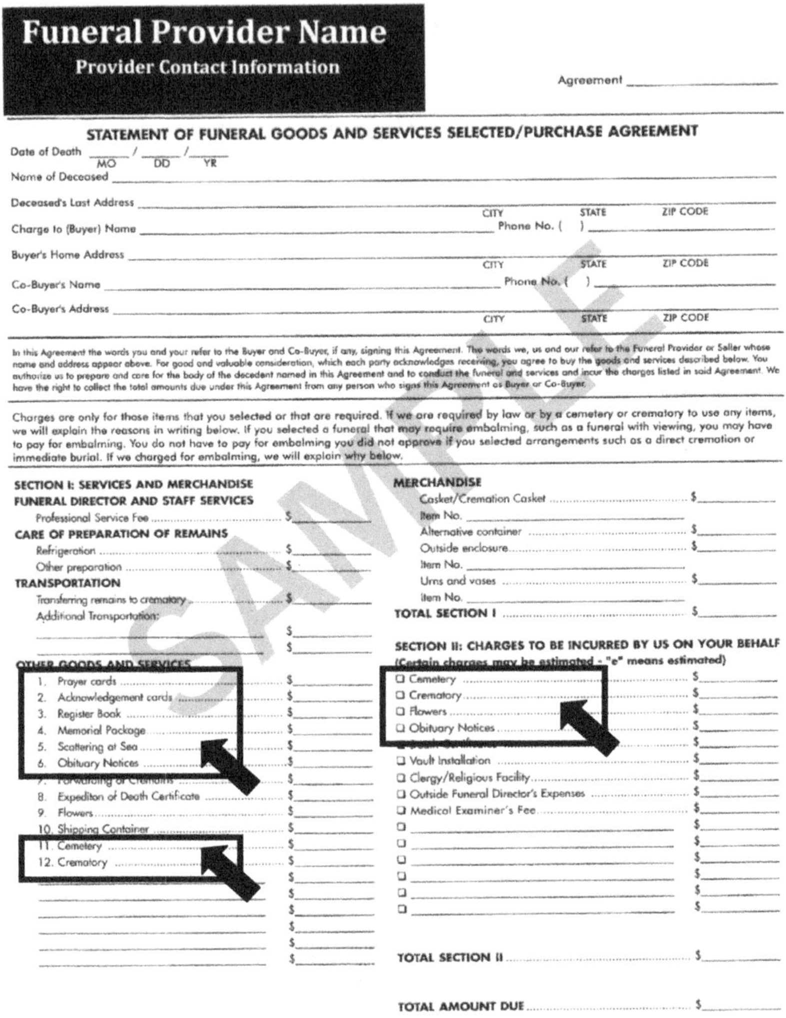

Funeral Provider Name
Provider Contact Information

Agreement ______

STATEMENT OF FUNERAL GOODS AND SERVICES SELECTED/PURCHASE AGREEMENT

Date of Death ___ / ___ / ___ (MO DD YR)

Name of Deceased ______

Deceased's Last Address ______ CITY STATE ZIP CODE

Charge to (Buyer) Name ______ Phone No. ( ) ______

Buyer's Home Address ______ CITY STATE ZIP CODE

Co-Buyer's Name ______ Phone No. ( ) ______

Co-Buyer's Address ______ CITY STATE ZIP CODE

In this Agreement the words you and your refer to the Buyer and Co-Buyer, if any, signing this Agreement. The words we, us and our refer to the Funeral Provider or Seller whose name and address appear above. For good and valuable consideration, which each party acknowledges receiving, you agree to buy the goods and services described below. You authorize us to prepare and care for the body of the decedent named in this Agreement and to conduct the funeral and services and incur the charges listed in said Agreement. We have the right to collect the total amounts due under this Agreement from any person who signs this Agreement as Buyer or Co-Buyer.

Charges are only for those items that you selected or that are required. If we are required by law or by a cemetery or crematory to use any items, we will explain the reasons in writing below. If you selected a funeral that may require embalming, such as a funeral with viewing, you may have to pay for embalming. You do not have to pay for embalming you did not approve if you selected arrangements such as a direct cremation or immediate burial. If we charged for embalming, we will explain why below.

SECTION I: SERVICES AND MERCHANDISE

FUNERAL DIRECTOR AND STAFF SERVICES

Professional Service Fee .... $____

CARE OF PREPARATION OF REMAINS

Refrigeration .... $____
Other preparation .... $____

TRANSPORTATION

Transferring remains to crematory .... $____
Additional Transportation: $____ $____

OTHER GOODS AND SERVICES

1. Prayer cards .... $____
2. Acknowledgement cards .... $____
3. Register Book .... $____
4. Memorial Package .... $____
5. Scattering at Sea .... $____
6. Obituary Notices .... $____
7. Forwarding of Cremains .... $____
8. Expedition of Death Certificate .... $____
9. Flowers .... $____
10. Shipping Container .... $____
11. Cemetery .... $____
12. Crematory .... $____

MERCHANDISE

Casket/Cremation Casket .... $____
Item No. ____
Alternative container .... $____
Outside enclosure .... $____
Item No. ____
Urns and vases .... $____
Item No. ____

TOTAL SECTION I .... $____

SECTION II: CHARGES TO BE INCURRED BY US ON YOUR BEHALF
(Certain charges may be estimated - "e" means estimated)

- ❑ Cemetery .... $____
- ❑ Crematory .... $____
- ❑ Flowers .... $____
- ❑ Obituary Notices .... $____
- ❑ Death Certificates .... $____
- ❑ Vault Installation .... $____
- ❑ Clergy/Religious Facility .... $____
- ❑ Outside Funeral Director's Expenses .... $____
- ❑ Medical Examiner's Fee .... $____

TOTAL SECTION II .... $____

TOTAL AMOUNT DUE .... $____

Sample funeral sales contract. Selections marked with arrows are items that you can do yourself or refuse to purchase from the funeral home to save money. There is an additional page to the contract with all disclaimers. *Read it thoroughly*.

Selecting a Funeral Provider

Many people look back at a funeral and regret how little time there was to make "the right choice" of funeral home, cemetery or crematory. Funeral providers furnish their facilities lavishly with expensive furniture and accessories to impress customers and mourners. They pump floral-scented air freshener through their venting system. They play quiet music. They speak in low tones. They wear business outfits and are perfectly groomed. They want you to be convinced of their value before you look at pricing.

Make your choice of provider based on four factors.

1. **Costs**. Your budget will determine which providers you will visit. If a provider looks too expensive ask early about their pricing. The law requires they give you their itemized General Price List before discussion. Many providers hand it out at the end of the meeting with marketing materials so you don't see the price sheet until you've left. Be prepared ahead of time to walk away from any funeral director who isn't

comfortable talking about pricing or who uses words you don't understand. You're not being rude if you walk away. You're being a smart shopper in a difficult situation.

2. **Reputation**. Ask family and friends. They'll have great feedback on which funeral home or provider to use.. and which ones not to use. Check on feedback from others who live in your area, too, with published feedback on web sites like Yelp!, Yahoo! and even Angie's List. Use an internet search term like **funeral home reviews** (and then the name of your city) to get the best results.

3. **Flexibility**. You may want to work with a company that will create the entire service for you. You may want to have a unique funeral outdoors, at a favorite hangout or somewhere else. Maybe grandpa would want to hold his favorite fishing rod. Maybe Aunt Jan wants her prized collection of tea cozies distributed to those gathered at the service. You're looking for a provider that can lead or follow depending upon your wishes.

4. **Gut level connection.** Find a provider who clicks with you and your needs.

What sales techniques should you be aware of at funeral providers?

When you visit a funeral home understand it's a business, and be aware of the following sales techniques used to influence how much you spend.

1. Funeral home staff will decide how much you're likely to spend when you walk in the front door based on how you look and how you dress. They may limit your options from the get-go to steer you toward the most expensive items they think you'll buy.

2. If you have an insurance policy you'll use for payment staff may discretely leave the room during your arrangements meeting (while you review selections, for instance) to verify the value of the policy. Verifying the policy tells them how much you can afford and some funeral directors will feel free to encourage you to spend it all. You may want to wait until the end of the meeting, after you agree on services and payment, to mention the insurance policy and how much it's worth. Note, too, that some unscrupulous providers

may tell you it will be easier to work with the insurance company if you sign over the rights to the policy payment to the funeral home. They may say the insurance funds will be moved more efficiently if they work directly with the insurer. Beware. Turning over the insurance policy gives the provider more control over how much is spent, especially on options or extras you might not expect or want. Most providers will write a contract to wait for insurance to be paid to you as long as they can verify the validity of the policy itself.

3. Funeral providers often use guilt to make families spend more. They use phrases like "the funeral your loved one deserves" to sell more expensive items. Typical shame-based phrases like "what he would want/expect" and “you wouldn’t want that to happen to mom, would you?” are aimed at twisting emotions to squeeze more money out of you. It can be difficult, but stick to your guns and get only the products and services you really want.

Tip #6

“Pre-paids” are items the funeral director buys on your behalf (unless you say you don’t want them) using your credit card. These items can add up fast.

4. The FTC requires that providers give you a GPL (general price list) that shows how much each item costs before you sign a contract. It runs three pages long and it must follow a specific format so you can compare one provider's GPL to another's. Ask for it early in your meeting. Some providers may steer you away from looking at GPL prices, telling you they have discounts that make it "simpler" to make your choices. Make sure you understand where "discounts" are figured into pricing – a discount on one item may mean overpaying on another. Funeral providers have wide profit margins. It can be easy for them to discount a casket by $1,000 when they already make a 300% profit from each one they sell. Your contract can look like a steal but be less than a good deal.

Use squints, "hmmms" and frowns to save money with providers. They want you to sign and will lower their prices if you look unhappy.

5. Package pricing is very popular. Some funeral homes make it look like they *only* have package pricing. Providers say packages help you get more value for your money and make the decisions about what to

include simpler. Some tell you the package is "complete" but there are almost always other required expenses. Take your time to fully understand what you're buying. While package pricing can appear to save money, often the price includes things you don't need or want. And in most cases item substitutions or deletions are not allowed in packages.

Package pricing often includes a flower allowance of $300, $400, or more. Funeral homes supply the flowers and assure you they're saving you time and money by making purchases for you. But those providers give you no opportunity to see the true price of the flowers they provide, and there is no refund if your flowers cost less than the "allowance" offers. Often neighborhood florists are your best bet, and creating simple arrangements yourself can help with your budget.

Tip #8

You can keep flower costs down by displaying objects tied to your loved one's hobbies, like a tackle box or gardening boots, and adding just a few blooms.

6. Casket shopping at the funeral home can feel like walking through a minefield. Casket pricing is hard to

compare from one provider to another -- many subtle differences in caskets can raise or lower prices drastically. The "discount" price at a high-end provider may still be more than the full price of the casket at an "economy" provider for the same unit.

Be wary especially of casket "sealers" and long casket durability guarantees, both of which the FTC says are largely unnecessary and of no use.

7. Funeral directors sometimes add lots of "extras" for the funeral. Some include guestbooks and programs that describe the service and discuss the life of the person who died. Others offer keepsake jewelry and mementos. Cremation providers even offer jewelry made from some of your loved one's ashes. These items can slip under your radar as costs are calculated, and you should watch for them.

   One budget-minded Atlanta provider says fancy registry books aren't worth the cost. He say no one looks at the book after a week or so, when thank-you's to funeral attendees have been written. He suggests a clean pad of paper instead.

8. Be clear on whether you want an obituary to run in local newspapers. Fewer families place an obituary today than in the past because our world is so much more connected. Far-flung mourners and creditors don't use newspapers to look for death listings in the

age of the internet.

If you want to write and place an obit in the newspaper yourself the funeral director may tell you the newspaper will refuse to run it if it isn't submitted by the funeral home. They may say newspaper staff can't be sure if your obit is real or a hoax if it isn't submitted by a trusted funeral professional. Don't be fooled -- you can write and place the obituary of your choice for much less than funeral homes generally charge.

Often enough, the obituary placed in the newspaper on your behalf by your funeral provider is simply a list of the information you provide for the death certificate, plus the name, logo and address of the funeral home itself. Some providers go so far as to use only the name of the deceased and display the company's logo and website address to send everyone to their website for more information. Paying for an obit through the funeral home can leave you feeling like you're running an ad for the funeral home.

If you write the obituary don't include home addresses or the time of the funeral. It tells thieves when you won't be home to interrupt them.

How strong are you when shopping? Do you ask for discounts or take what's offered? Who can you take with you to help out?

pamphlet back

fold line

"Oh heart, if one should say to you that the soul perishes like the body, answer that the flower withers, but the seed remains."
~Kahlil Gibran

pamphlet front

In
Loving Memory

Bessie Harlow
February 23, 1928 - March 14, 2002

inside left

fold line

Let us together celebrate the life of
Bessie Harlow
February 23, 1928 - March 14, 2002

Call to Worship
Opening Prayer
Reading of the 23rd Psalm (All)

The Lord is my shepherd; I shall not want.
He makes me lie down in green pastures.
He leads me beside still waters.
He restores my soul.
He leads me in paths of righteousness
for his name's sake.

Even though I walk through the valley
of the shadow of death,
I will fear no evil,
for you are with me;
your rod and your staff,
they comfort me.
You prepare a table before me
in the presence of my enemies;
you anoint my head with oil;
my cup overflows.
Surely goodness and mercy shall follow me
all the days of my life,
and I shall dwell in the house of the Lord
forever.

inside right

Scripture Reading
Song of Tribute
Prayer

Our Father in heaven,
hallowed be your name.
Your kingdom come,
your will be done,
on earth, as it is in heaven.
Give us this day our daily bread,
and forgive us our debts,
as we also have forgiven our debtors.
And lead us not into temptation,
but deliver us from evil.
For thine is the kingdom,
the power, and the glory.
Amen

Hymn: Be Still My Soul, number 242
Benediction
Recessional Music

Sample of a funeral program you or your kids can make and print at home.

The casket

Caskets are hard to shop for. Manufacturers often use the same name as other manufacturers for caskets that are very different. A manufacturer may name several products by the same name, each one a bit different than the others. Prices among the lookalikes can vary by several thousand dollars.

Casket selection can be truly overwhelming. Do you want something simple or something with lots of scroll work? Do you want the optional 3-D corner pieces? Is the interior fabric texture important? Which satin will look good with your loved one's skin tone?

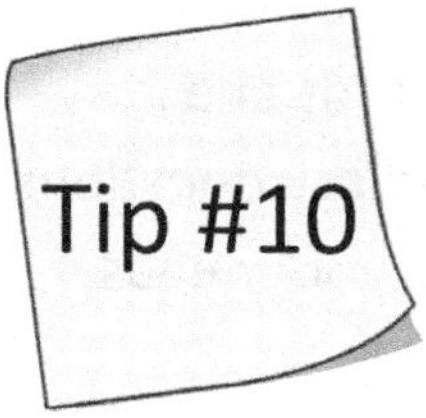

Check out our website before you shop to make some initial choices without the pressure of a salesperson trailing behind you at **http://usfuneralcosts.com/casket-styles/**.

Give yourself a set amount of time to decide whether you'd like a dark or light wood casket, a steel casket of a certain color (many models come in a variety of colors), or even a cloth-covered or simple pine casket (the least expensive).

It makes sense to look at caskets in person at the funeral home even if you don't expect to buy one there. Funeral directors adjust pricing in their head throughout your arrangements meeting, which includes the time you spend looking at caskets. You may get a bigger overall discount if they think you'll be buying something impressive. Use the time in the selection room to touch caskets, note their prices and even take pictures.

Don't be fooled by casket guarantees displayed with caskets. How will you know if the guarantee is worth it if you can't see the results without spending thousands of dollars to check on it?

After looking at caskets at the funeral home, buying online can be a great way to save money. There are thousands of caskets online, and looking at caskets in person will help you know what you're looking for before you shop the web. The best online casket sellers have established track records and reviews from past customers. Read reviews and ask questions of each seller until you find one you feel meets your needs.

What are caskets made of?

Most caskets sold here are made in the US or China. Often US and Chinese caskets are nearly identical but the US-made models cost more because labor and materials cost more in the US than in China.

A few large companies provide most of the caskets that are made in US. They each own a group of casket manufacturers who sell similar products at different price points.

The majority of caskets are made of wood and wood veneers, steel, copper, bronze, and even, in a tiny number of cases, gold. The most expensive gold casket I've seen costs $259,000 and comes with a bust (head and shoulders statue) keepsake of the loved one who died.

Gold casket with additional inner lid. List price $259,000

Of standard casket selections, *solid wood caskets* are more expensive and can be described as "better" than wood-veneer models, but in the end the casket is needed for only a few days before burial. Wood veneer is a thin layer of real wood glued over basic components like particle board. A mahogany veneer can be stained and finished to look like old world mahogany for much less money than the cost of a solid mahogany unit. You can have a beautiful casket for a fraction of the cost.

Typically, select woods (poplar, willow) will be the least expensive wood caskets, followed by pine, oak, birch, maple, cherry, black walnut and mahogany.

Steel caskets are made from differing thicknesses of rolled steel. The gauge (a number that indicates how thick the steel is) indicates how many layers of this particular steel it would take to make a stack one inch tall. Most caskets come in 20, 18 and 16 gauge. 16 gauge is the thickest and usually the most expensive.

Stainless steel caskets are often more expensive than plain steel in the same way kitchen appliances made of stainless steel are more expensive than others. They're sold as rust-resistant but that claim can only be backed up by opening the grave over time.

Copper and bronze caskets are defined by their weight, labeled in ounces. A 32-oz. copper or bronze casket means that the copper or bronze used weighs 32 ounces per square foot. Heavier is more expensive. A 48 ounce bronze model is marketed as “better quality” than 32 ounce model.

Other factors that affect casket cost include the type and style of siderails and ornamentation. Painted, stamped steel is the least expensive, while die-cast hardware that has been buffed and polished by hand is among the most expensive. Some hardware that looks like metal may be manufactured from plastics so the casket can be less pricey and still look expensive.

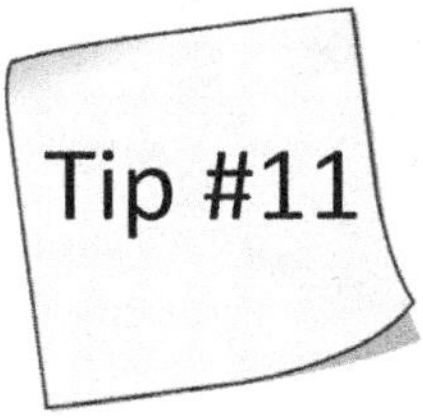

Don’t purchase a casket for a cremation. Rent a casket from the funeral home for under $1,500 a day if you think it’s important, but a two-day rental is as expensive as a purchase.

In the end the least expensive caskets, which are made of pine, veneer, oak or fabric-over-particleboard will do less to pollute the environment than the fancier models and will work just as well for the short time they’re needed.

Caskets are also sold by CostCo and Walmart.

Alternative caskets

Pictured below are some low-cost alternative caskets and a shroud. I particularly like the *"Return To Sender"* casket. I found them on **www.memorials.com**, a family business.

What kind of casket to do you want? Wood? Metal? An alternative casket made from heavy cardboard? A willow basket?

How do funeral staff influence which casket you'll buy?

The funeral director will show you several caskets during your arrangements meeting. The funeral home will have a room full of models on display. You will be steered toward a small group of caskets based on what the staff thinks you can afford.

Tip #12

Salespeople know customers don't want to look at caskets at all, and know that by the third option most customers are overwhelmed.

Sales techniques are learned in funeral services school, at funeral directors' conventions and on the job as an apprentice.

A classic casket sales technique is to show you a model that's cheaper than you can afford first (this can be a casket that's not polished as nicely as others, that's placed too high off the floor for you to get a good look at, or not lit as well), then a casket that's clearly too expensive, and lastly a casket priced in the middle. This third one is the one they want you to buy.

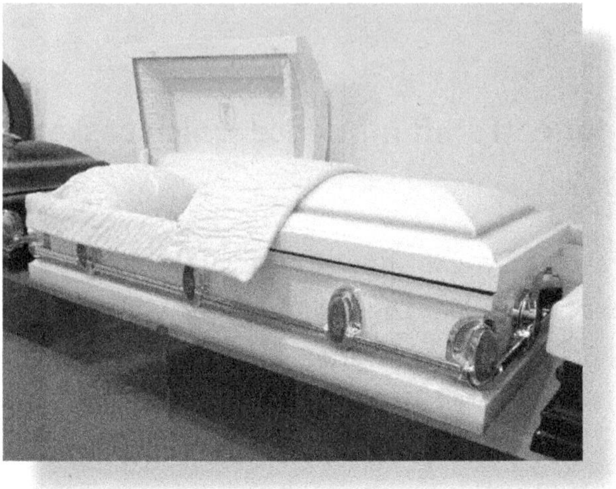

How can you avoid sales tactics? Know exactly what you can afford. Be wary of casket discounts. If you get a discount on the casket you'll probably pay more in other fees and expenses to balance it out. Remember that funeral providers are business people and their job is to make a profit.

Don't feel guilty asking for bigger discounts. Funeral homes typically spend $300 or less for every $1,000 they charge on caskets, so they have plenty of room for negotiations. I used a simple frown when looking at an estimated bill at one funeral home and the sales person snatched the contract back, stepped out of the room and returned with an additional $1,000 discount I hadn't asked for.

What should you be thinking about when choosing a casket?

Funeral providers want you to think the casket you choose is a symbol of how you feel about the person you're burying and a way of impressing the neighbors. The funeral industry would like you to think that heavier bronze caskets, thicker steel caskets and solid wood caskets are worth more because they will protect the body better over time.

In the end you will need the casket for the days after the death and before you bury your loved one. After burial no one will see the casket. No one can guarantee it without digging it up in the future to prove its worth. The government says guarantees are worthless.

Your casket choice is very much like the choice of which car to buy: an inexpensive hatch-back model and a top of the line SUV will both get you where you want to go. If you feel an expensive model is for you and you have the money, spend the money. If you're on a budget buy something less expensive and use the remaining money to help others come in from out of town for the service.

What's a sealer or gasket and why doesn't it work?

Your funeral provider may suggest that you buy a casket with a "sealer" or "gasket." The two words describe the same thing: a flexible rubber tube that runs around the top edge of the casket bottom, like the one on your refrigerator door that compresses to form a seal to keep cold air in and warmer air out.

Your funeral director may tell you the sealer/gasket will keep the elements out of the casket (water in the case of a flood, or tree roots and bugs) by creating an air-tight seal between the bottom and the top of the container. Some funeral providers will tell you this tight seal helps to preserve the body much longer than an unsealed casket.

The law forbids claims that these features help preserve the remains longer or indefinitely because they don't. The FTC says sealers and gaskets are completely unnecessary. They just add to the cost of the funeral. Gaskets and sealers cost under $20 to make but sell for $600 - $800. Avoid them.

Another lesser-known, yucky-but-true fact: sealing the casket air-tight traps gases created by bacteria that thrive in environments where there is no air. These gases may cause extreme pressure, and a small number of caskets have split open under the pressure.

If you buy a casket with a sealer or gasket you may wish to cut an end section of the sealer off before it's closed for the last time so gases can escape.

Are caskets guaranteed?

The FTC Rule of 1984 is very specific on this issue. You should expect a guarantee that the casket the funeral home delivers will be the model you paid for, in good condition without scratches or dents, and that it will open, close and lock as expected. But no manufacturer can guarantee a casket will help preserve the body over a long time.

A casket's true purpose is to easily store and move the body until it's buried or cremated. Caskets, sealers, burial vaults and grave liners cannot legally be guaranteed to protect and preserve. Don't let a funeral home imply that your guarantee covers more than it does.

Is it safe to buy a casket online? How much can I save?

Funeral home salespeople may tell you an online casket can arrive damaged and they won't be able to repair it. They may tell you some caskets never arrive. These are very rare problems when buying on the internet, but they do happen to a very small number of buyers.

You can save thousands of dollars by purchasing a casket for the funeral at an online seller. If you have a style of casket you like you can find the same model or something that looks very similar but is made of different materials and save up to 70% of the price you'd pay at a funeral home.

Tip #13

Make sure your online source displays prices and shipping costs clearly. Make sure they offer 24-hour a day service.

A "prestigious" solid mahogany casket model costs between eight thousand and nine thousand dollars at funeral homes, but you can get a lookalike mahogany-veneered casket (veneer is a thin layer of wood over other materials) that essentially looks as beautiful and functions the same as the $9,000 model for around $1,500, plus $300 overnight shipping, online.

You can search for casket sellers on the web with the search terms **caskets online**.

Ask online sellers what will happen if the casket arrives damaged. Pay for the insurance they offer if it makes sense to you.

A cautionary tale

A small number of online purchases don't go well. The casket pictured below, purchased online, arrived damaged. The locks didn't work. The buyer called the online seller and the seller said they would do nothing to fix the problem. The funeral provider could have sold the family a new casket at list price, but because the funeral home knew the family well (it was my family this happened to, actually) staff went to a local arts and crafts store and bought sticky-backed Velcro that was used to attach the top of the casket to the base before the casket was loaded into the hearse for transport to the cemetery. It was upsetting for family members.

Because the casket was placed directly in a vault at the cemetery the buyer knew the makeshift solution would work for the short time it was needed.

The seller offered no refund. Luckily, the buyer used a credit card to buy the casket online. The credit card company refunded the full cost of the casket.

What are your weaknesses when buying big-ticket items? How can you prepare to avoid being taken advantage of?

How do online flower prices stack up?

Shopping for flowers is simple and complicated at the same time. The best (and most time-consuming) way to compare arrangements is to look at product descriptions to find the number of blooms in each arrangement, the size (measured in inches) of each arrangement, and check out the pictures to see if a "better" bouquet at one seller is equal to or better than a "best" arrangement on another site, but that takes a lot of work.

Funeral homes often sell floral arrangements and while it's the most convenient way to buy it's the most expensive way to purchase. Flowers from a funeral home have two mark-ups – one from the florist who created them and one from the funeral home. The funeral home does not add a charge for accepting flowers on your behalf but the florists will charge for delivery.

Some funeral homes link directly to other website florists on their own site, but the up-charges can be steep.

Local florists can be less expensive but delivery charges may be $25 or more depending on location (online services will have delivery charges, too). Compare local florist reviews on the web using search terms like **funeral flowers review** (then the name of your city).

The major florist web sites have been on the web for years and they're easy to find. The difficulty comes when you want to compare a floral arrangement at one site to a similar or "same" arrangement at another site.

The trend online is to sell 3 levels of any arrangement, usually "good," "better" and "best." Each level has more flowers or more of the key blooms and each level costs more.

Your first choice in flowers should be to decide on your budget. Once you've come up with a number, search for **funeral flowers under** (then enter your price) on the web.

On the next page you'll find a funeral wreath sold by three online vendors. All are simple white wreaths. The wreaths use a combination of daisies, chrysanthemums or roses (the number of each type of flower sets the price) but all of them look very similar, and for the cost conscious, the least expensive looks as good as the most expensive. And is just as meaningful.

Link 1
http://www.1800flowers.com/white-standing-wreath

Link 2 http://www.fromyouflowers.com/products/1-800-flowers_white_standing_wreath.htm

Link 3
https://www.ftd.com/the-ftd-splendor-wreath

Take a look at **http://usfuneralcosts.com/floral-arrangements/** to see pricing on popular floral arrangements.

Take a look at **http://usfuneralcosts.com/make-your-own-funeral-floral-arrangements/** to learn about making your own floral arrangements. You may not feel talented enough to create your own bouquet or wreath, but someone in your family might love the opportunity to show their love.

Gardening boot and faux daisies. I created it for under $20, in under 20 minutes.

What color(s) of flowers would you like? Do you want chrysanthemums and roses or will daisies serve the same purpose? What hobbies could you incorporate into the arrangement?

Selecting a cemetery

If you're an honorably-discharged veteran you're entitled to a free grave, opening and closing, vault and marker, plus a free grave for your spouse in a national veterans' cemetery.

If you're not a veteran you'll have a lot of decisions to make, starting with which cemetery you want to use. Select a cemetery based on the following considerations:

1. **Costs**. Ownership of the cemetery plays a big role in pricing. Non-profits and city or municipal cemeteries generally have the lowest prices, followed by independently owned and then corporate-owned cemeteries.

2. **Distance**. If someone will visit frequently think about how they'll travel to the location. Family car? Public transport? If, after thinking about it for a bit, no one will likely visit regularly and the people who do visit have transportation, distance can be less important and the best prices may be across town.

3. **Space**. Will other family members be buried in nearby graves? Sometimes there are discounts for multiple plots but beware of "deals" -- one cemetery I visited was running a "head of household" promotion. The head of household received their grave site free with the purchase of plots for other family members who would be buried there in the future. The additional gravesites were more expensive than usual to make up for lost income.

4. **Cemetery features**. You may want a quiet neighborhood location. You may want to be buried in a historic cemetery. You may want to be buried inexpensively or in an environmentally sound "green" cemetery. It's entirely up to you.

What makes a cemetery the right choice for you? What are your priorities?

What standard fees can be expected at cemeteries?

Your contract with a cemetery includes the gravesite and much more.

Example of the typical costs of burial (item definitions start on the next page):

Gravesite (plot) $2,500
Vault $1,100
Vault installation $400
Opening and closing $1,300
Marker $1,200
Marker installation $400

Ask about ongoing fees. Some cemeteries charge for maintenance when the grave is purchased. Others charge a continuing maintenance fee.

There may be different maintenance levels throughout the cemetery. A cemetery on the north side of Atlanta that charges from $2,000 to $2,000,000 for grave sites waters the lawns of the more expensive plots with an in-ground watering system and hand-trims the grass. The less expensive plots rely on rain for watering and are mowed with a tractor that rolls over everything in wide cuts. This tractor-style mowing is the reason that many cemeteries require flat headstones (which are called “markers”) for the less expensive plots.

Definitions of terms used at cemeteries:

The vault is a cement shoebox-shaped container the casket is placed in during burial. It has a base and a top (lid). The weight of the lid “seals” the box.

Vaults with metal inner shells and bank vault style “doors” instead of top cement slabs can cost thousands of dollars more but cannot be guaranteed to protect the contents better than a basic model.

A burial liner is a heavy-duty plastic box with no bottom that fits over the sides and top of the casket after the casket is laid in place. Many cemeteries do not allow burial liners.

Both come in a wide range of prices. Basic units can be purchased for around $800. Ask about installation fees. Some cemeteries charge hundreds of dollars to place the vault into the grave. The average cost for installation is $400.

Tip #14

Don’t let cemetery sales people talk you into buying a more expensive vault than the least expensive one – The law says they can’t claim one will do a better job than the other.

Federal and state laws do not require a vault or liner, and funeral providers are not allowed to tell you otherwise. Most cemeteries, however, require some type of outer burial container (vault or liner) to prevent the grave from sinking in the future as the casket and contents decay. Neither grave liners nor burial vaults are capable of preventing the eventual decomposition of human remains.

A simple concrete vault ready for burial

Opening and closing of the grave -- digging the hole and setting up the tent and chairs for the service and replacing the soil and sod after burial -- can be the second largest expense after the plot itself.

Expect higher opening/closing fees – referred to by funeral providers as “O/C” -- at some cemeteries for providing extra chairs for the service if you decide to have the entire funeral service at the grave (which is much less expensive than having a chapel service first, in most cases).

The memorial (a stone or plaque that lies flat) or headstone (a stone that stands upright) can be costly. It may even cost more than some gravesites. Watch out for cemetery salespeople who use guilt or shame tactics to pressure you into buying a more expensive stone.

A standard monument.

An upgraded monument with a floral design can cost thousands more.

Some cemeteries include the stone, stone installation and stone maintenance in a single fee, but not all do.

Some cemeteries will tell you that if you choose to provide your own stone and the stone is damaged you'll be responsible for making repairs immediately, even if you live far from the cemetery. This is generally a ploy to keep you from buying a monument over the internet.

Some cemeteries offer a brass bud vase attached to the stone (at a premium price) for displaying flowers, but if you're not going to be regularly placing flowers skip the vase.

Some cemeteries offer annual flower packages that will place new flowers on the grave every month, but you can spend less if you do it yourself and make it more meaningful by bringing flowers from the garden.

Do I own the burial plot/land/site I buy at the cemetery?

No. You're buying *the legal right to use the space* to bury the body there, but you're not buying the land itself.

The cemetery owners have an agreement with the local government that the land the cemetery sits on will be "held in perpetuity" (used forever) as a cemetery and they make commitments to maintain the land in the future.

Tip #15

Cemeteries pass on the costs of maintaining the cemetery to the families of those who are buried there.

What's the reason some graves are so much more expensive in the same cemetery?

Most cemeteries divide their grounds into sections. Sections have groups of plots. Sections may have themes, may serve specific religions, or feature "views" of fountains or ponds.

Costlier sections offer nicer landscaping, include better maintenance or offer gated privacy. Family "estates," where several members of the same family are buried next to one another, can be surprisingly expensive.

Note that “family estates” are not the same as buying standard plots next to one another, which can be an economical way to make sure the family will be buried together over time. Estate plots usually have other “features” such as trees, statues, oversize monuments, gates, chapels and prime locations.

The least expensive lots in a cemetery are generally those near the entrance or near busy streets at the edges of the grounds.

What's a mausoleum?

A mausoleum is a building on the cemetery grounds used as an alternative to in-ground burial. Mausoleums provide spaces for caskets (columbariums offer space for cremation remains).

Tip #16

"Double" mausoleum spaces hold two caskets so couples can be laid to rest together over time.

Some mausoleums have spaces inside and outside the building.

You might think mausoleums would be less expensive than graves but that's not generally true. Cemeteries sell mausoleums as "prestigious" and "better at the preservation" of the body because the space is off the ground and is usually under an eave of some kind "so it can withstand bad weather."

Cemetery salespeople may say a mausoleum makes the loved one easier to visit, even in rain or snow.

Mausoleum "niches" (individual spaces) are usually stacked six to eight high. The niches at eye level are the most expensive, followed by the niches at waist level and then the niches at knee level. The niches at the top (one cemetery calls them "the penthouse") can cost half as much as lower niches.

Although vaults are not required in a mausoleum, opening and closing costs are much the same as for in-ground burial.

Generally speaking all markers at a mausoleum look the same. Some cemeteries offer individual optional bud vases.

Caskets sealers are not allowed in mausoleums because of the internal pressure the gases can create.

Why does a burial after 3pm often cost so much more?

Burial services that start late in the day could require staff to work past regular operating hours, which means overtime charges for the cemetery managers.

Cemeteries claim that any burial that begins after 3pm has a higher chance of incurring additional staffing costs, so services that start at 3pm or later can cost more in anticipation of increased staff costs regardless of whether workers are held over.

Can I put a spouse's or pet's ashes in the casket with my loved one before burial?

I ask this question when I "mystery shop" providers. The answer often depends on whether the provider is owned by a national corporation or owned by a family locally.

Locally-owned funeral homes will most often say they don't ask for an inventory of what goes in the casket before they close it for the last time.

Corporate-owned and "chain" funeral homes are more likely to say they have an additional recordkeeping fee because they are required (by the company) to track the final disposition of cremains, even cremains that were never in their custody. They imply the fee is specified by law, but it's not.

I was once told that if I wanted to bury cremains in a casket with a loved one's body I would need to buy an additional memorial or headstone, plus a second plot. The total fee quoted was more than the original gravesite itself.

How can I save money on a cemetery plot?

There's a place to buy everything online and in the case of cemetery plots there are websites that offer discounted individual or family graves across the country. These are called plot "re-sales." **Www.Craigslist.org** has national listings, but try a simple search on your computer using the terms **buy a cemetery plot** along with your city name to find listings in your area.

In essence, cemetery plot re-sales happen when someone purchased a site in the past and now, for whatever reason, they won't be using it. They may have moved across the country. They may have decided on cremation. They list it for sale at a discount to take it off their hands.

A new cemetery management team can mean big cemetery price hikes over time and "re-sales" can save you a lot of money. Often enough, the original owner of the plot bought when the cemetery was under different ownership a long time ago. Now it's owned by a multi-state corporation that raised prices by a few thousand dollars when it took over.

I saw one instance where the original owner bought the plot for $1,000 twenty years ago. Until six months ago the price (before a management change) had risen to $2,995. The current price with the new cemetery owners is $4,995. The original plot owner was selling for just $800 because the plot was part of an estate that needed to be settled.

Generally speaking you'll see ads that offer to sell the lot and to pay the deed transfer costs. The deed is part of the contract signed between the cemetery and plot buyers. You will sign a new contract with the cemetery, which will include your new deed. There may be other related fees for the transfer.

Tip #17

Even with a "re-sale" you'll need to pay for the opening, the closing, the vault and the marker.

Follow the tips below to make sure your purchase will be legal and clear of problems. *Note: The author of this book is not an attorney. Check with your lawyer to verify details.*

Go out to the cemetery to see lots you've found on the internet. If you're not in the area ask the cemetery to email you a map of the cemetery so you can see exactly where the plot is located. Have them verify the current price in that section so you know what kind of price break you're getting.

Look at how long the lot has been available – you might be

able to negotiate an even lower price to take it off the owner's hands.

Tip #18

Verify the gravesite is not in use and is actually owned by the seller with a call to the cemetery office.

Some of the sites that offer to re-sell gravesites are run by brokers who sell the property for the actual owner and charge a percentage to handle all the paperwork. Not all brokers have the best motivations or intentions. Don't buy without knowing exactly who you're dealing with and what you're getting.

Some web sites that re-sell cemetery lots for private owners and cemeteries:

www.craigslist.org/ mostly private sales

http://www.thecemeteryexchange.com/ broker and private sales

http://www.finalarrangementsnetwork.com/ broker site, cemetery may be seller

http://www.plotexchange.com/ broker and private sales

http://www.gravesolutions.com/ may be duplicate listings from other web sites

The author of this book is not responsible for the accuracy or availability of lots sold as private sales or as brokered sales over the internet or through local ads.

Can I choose to bury my loved one on my own property?

Some states allow it and some don't. Some that allow it require you to have an acre or more land or to put in a driveway that allows the public to access the grave at all times. Check with your county. Be prepared to disclose the grave(s) to anyone you sell the land to.

If your state and county allow the burial, know that you have the option in the future to disinter (move the remains to another location) if you sell the property.

Do veterans have special burial rights?

All veterans are entitled to a free burial in a national cemetery and a free grave marker. This eligibility also extends to some civilians who have provided military-related service and some public health service personnel.

The Florida National Cemetery in Bushnell, Florida

There are no charges for opening or closing the grave, for a vault or liner, or for installing the marker in a national cemetery.

Spouses and dependent children also are entitled to a burial spot and a marker when buried in a national cemetery but the family is responsible for opening and closing, a vault if necessary, marker and transportation to the cemetery.

National cemeteries are highly regulated. Graves are dug and used one next to the other in the order they're needed. There are often no gravesite location choices or any marker selections.

Tip #19

National cemeteries usually offer columbarium spaces for cremains as an alternative to traditional burial.

You may see ads for so-called "veterans' specials" by commercial cemeteries: these cemeteries may offer a free plot for the veteran, but overcharge for an adjoining plot for the spouse, and charge high fees for opening and closing each grave. Evaluate the bottom-line cost to be sure the "special" is as special as you may be led to believe.

Can I buy my own marker/memorial for the grave?

The simple answer is yes, you can, but each cemetery has rules about whether they allow it and what they'll charge to install it. You can save up to 50% online but not all cemeteries will be happy to accommodate you – basic headstones that cost only $400 over the internet generally cost about $1,200 when purchased through the cemetery, and they don't want to lose the profit they'll make.

Some cemeteries will do their best to make it difficult for you to use a headstone purchased online. They may charge an extra fee for installing the marker. They may charge for maintenance (an annual cleaning for example). They may tell you they will not notify you if the headstone is cracked, or, on the other hand, they may demand that you repair the headstone (even if you're in another state) with very little notice, and then charge you fees for installing a replacement.

Your cemetery notes:

Cremation

Cremation is the act of burning the remains using very high heat in an enclosed area. The body is placed in the "retorte" in a heavy-duty cardboard container or a canvas bag and everything is reduced to ashes in a few hours. Toxic fumes from embalming fluids, dentistry, a casket and other sources are electronically cleaned out of the exhaust air before the air is released into the environment. Older crematorium filtration systems may not clean the air as well as new ones.

Tip #20

Don't buy a casket for cremation. Use an "alternative container" made of cardboard, fabric or wood.

Some crematories allow the family to see the body a last time and to be present for the cremation for an additional charge. A few crematories have a chapel for services onsite.

Ashes can be returned to family members who wait for them. Ashes are generally returned to the family by the funeral director within a week.

Actual cremation may be delayed and the body held for up to a week by local authorities if there are questions about the cause of death to ensure an investigation can be completed beforehand.

The law says only one body can be cremated in the chamber at a time. This rule ensures the ashes returned to the family are only those of the deceased and allows simpler identification using forensic tools later if required (although ashes are difficult to identify). The cremation chamber (retorte) is cleaned between uses.

Pacemakers must be removed before cremation because there is a risk of explosion of the batteries. Funeral home or crematory staff can take care of this for you.

Be aware that jewelry and other small metal objects will melt during cremation and cannot be returned after cremation. Larger objects like hip replacement devices will be returned on request. Creepy, but true.

Ashes and bones (the cremains) are ground into small bits after burning and look like gritty sand. If no urn is pre-selected by the family to hold the remains, ashes are returned to the family in a plastic bag inside a cardboard or plastic box with an ID tag that was placed in the burning unit with the body.

What's the difference between a "traditional" cremation, a "memorial service" and a "direct" cremation?

The body of the deceased is present for a **traditional cremation service**, and the service itself is very much like any other traditional funeral service. The body is either in a simple and inexpensive casket that will be cremated with the body or is in a rental casket the funeral home provides.

A rental casket has an end that opens to allow the body and the container it's in to be removed after services. A rental casket from the funeral home costs $1,000 - $1,500 a day to rent. The rental casket is sanitized between burials.

Rental caskets cost funeral providers about $2,500. The casket is destroyed after 25 – 30 uses. Profit on rentals is huge.

The body is not present for a cremation **memorial service** and the service may be held at any time, even months after death. A remembrance (memorial) service can be held anywhere – outdoors, at a favorite dining or drinking spot (this one's a lot less formal), or as part of a family reunion.

A **direct cremation** is very simple and the most cost-effective: the body is removed from the place of death, no formal memorial services are held, and ashes are returned to the family a few days to a week later. It should cost no more than $1,000, and is often less.

My father wanted a direct cremation. His body was removed from the house within hours of death. Those hours gave me time to sit with him, call the family, and to say goodbye. This window of time can be an opportunity for closure for you, too.

The family gathered for my father's memorial service several months later. We rented a house for a long weekend. It had room for everyone to sleep, had a pool, and was close to shopping and the beach. I brought all the items I knew someone would want from the house and placed them in the center of a very big dining table. We talked about the items and each person took home what was meaningful to them.

Our time together and our shared memories were worth so much more than a formal funeral, yet cost less than a simple funeral and burial would have cost.

Why do more and more people select cremation over burial?

Cremation is thought to be better for the environment than burial because there is no metal from a casket left in the ground, no cement vault or grave liner left to leech chemicals into the ground, no graveyard chemical lawn maintenance or the run-off it causes, and no land used.

Direct cremation is simple and inexpensive and leaves family and friends as much time as they need to plan a meaningful memorial service since there is no rush to bury the body.

What does the Funeral Rule say about direct cremation?

Under the Funeral Rule, funeral directors who offer direct cremations may not tell you that state or local law requires a wooden, metal or other expensive casket for cremations, because none do.

Funeral homes must disclose in writing your right to buy an *alternative container* (a heavy cardboard box or simple pine box) for a direct cremation. Alternative containers generally start at $150. You may wish to consider a shroud.

Metal caskets are prohibited from cremation chambers. If a funeral director sells you a metal casket for the cremation it helps their bottom line but it doesn't help you. The law requires that metal caskets be destroyed and discarded at a crematory before the body is cremated.

Where can ashes be spread?

It varies from state to state. National parks allow it in some areas but it must be scheduled. Check with state parks for the rules. Most local public parks allow it if you are respectful of others.

You can pour the ashes into a river, lake or the ocean. You can release them on your property. You can scatter them in a nearby private woods if the owner has given consent.

You can put the ashes in a memorial container (urn) and set them in a favorite place in your home.

Tip #21

A well-known writer had his ashes put into fireworks and set off over his ranch several years ago.

You can have jewelry made with ashes sealed inside. Some funeral home staff sell these accessories as items that help keep your loved one close to your heart.

The sky's the limit – some people even have their ashes sent to space.

If you want to take the cremains to another city or country know that ashes are allowed on planes but you must have the paperwork that came with the ashes to verify the contents when travelling.

Alternatives to traditional burial and cremation

"Green" burial is growing in popularity and is said to be healthier for the environment than traditional burial. Green cemeteries do not allow embalming before burial. Wood or woven caskets and shrouds are acceptable coverings for the body at burial. Metal parts, and in most cases, jewelry are not permitted to be buried. The body, the fabric and other biodegradable items return to the soil.

How is green burial different from a traditional burial?

The essence of the "green" burial philosophy is the encouragement of the decomposition that happens naturally whenever a body is buried, but without the waste and toxins that can leech into the ground at a "standard" cemetery. Green burial eliminates most of the materials and chemicals that go into traditional burial by prohibiting embalming, vaults and grave liners, metal, and non-natural casket materials.

Green cemeteries often keep the landscaping in a natural state, often with meadows, hills or forest.

Green cemeteries generally cost much less than traditional cemeteries.

Opening and closing the grave is generally less expensive, and it's not unusual for families and friends to roll up their sleeves and re-fill the grave themselves with shovels as a meaningful way to say goodbye.

"Natural" woodsy cemetery

Gravesites at green cemeteries are sometimes marked with simple ground plaques, but some cemeteries allow no markers. If no markers are allowed mourners are given the geo-coordinates of where the grave is located so they can find the grave using their phone when visiting in the future.

"Pasture-like" green cemetery

Some green cemeteries allow plantings on the grave, some do not.

What does green burial cost vs traditional cemetery burial?

A traditional funeral with a service at the funeral home, a mid-range casket, flowers, embalming and other body care, a hearse and a cemetery plot with a view can cost $15,000.

A comparable green burial, with a simple wooden casket, required body cleaning, funeral home fees, a few floral arrangements (or even plants that will be installed at the grave), transportation to the green cemetery and a nice plot can cost $7,000 or less.

See **www.greenburialcouncil.org** for information about green cemeteries in your area.

Are you interested in green burial? What kind of green cemetery would you want to be buried in?

Can you have a funeral at home without help from a funeral provider?

There is a new trend in funerals called home funerals. In essence, the family keeps the body and home, creates their own services and decorates a pine or cardboard casket, and in some cases takes the casket to the cemetery or crematory themselves.

Some funeral directors may say that keeping the body at home is dangerous or unpleasant due to decomposition, but national law says using dry ice to cool the body at home is as acceptable as using the funeral home's refrigerator.

No embalming is required to keep the body at home before burial.

There are nine states that require you to use a funeral director no matter what you plan to do after a death. The funeral industry oversees the state laws that determine what must or can be done, and they don't want to lose business.

You can generally keep the body at home in those states but the funeral director you work with may require that a member of their staff is present 24 hours a day at an extra fee. Funeral directors in those states say they require it because they have taken legal custody of the body and must ensure that everything is done according to the law.

The other 41 states allow you to take care of the body yourself and hold the funeral at home with a family member selected as "funeral director."

There are professional and thoughtful home funeral "guides" who can help the family walk through everything that needs to be done. Go to **www.homefuneralalliance.org** to find someone near you.

The key elements of a home funeral are:

Washing and dressing the body after death and laying the body in a place of honor where friends and family can spend time saying goodbye anytime, day or night.

Dry ice or refrigeration beginning no later than 24 hours after death are the minimum legal requirements for keeping the body in good condition. Dry ice, wrapped in towels to keep the core body temperature cool but not frozen, is placed underneath the torso for a home funeral, and more is added as needed. You can find detailed instructions at **www.homefuneralalliance.org.**

Creating the Service and Decorating the casket using familiar objects and meaningful memorials is the chief advantage to having a home funeral. Favorite objects, blankets, or flowers from the garden add personal touches. Asking everyone to pitch in to decorate the casket (often a heavy cardboard box) before taking the body to a green cemetery or a crematory is a wonderful way to send best wishes with the body.

Tip #22

Creating a meaningful farewell service is a special benefit of home funerals. The entire family and all friends can choose how to say goodbye in their own way.

If you want to know more about home funerals
I strongly suggest you watch the video called
"A Family Undertaking" on Netflix or Youtube.com

What are financial reasons to have a funeral in your own home?

If you're willing to do the legwork to get the death certificate, which involves picking up forms from your county health department and taking those forms to the doctor in charge at the end of your loved one's life (this can take several trips), and you have your own land for burial, a funeral in your own home with a home-built pine or cardboard casket (you can buy cardboard units online or get one from a crematory) can cost under $500.

A home funeral with cremation can cost under $800 but you need to get a permit from the county to transport the body from your home to the crematory (and you need an SUV or truck bed large enough to accommodate the casket).

It can be a good idea to work with a professional funeral director for death certificate, transportation and permits. The cost should be no more than $500 for those 3 services.

The real benefits of home funerals are emotional, but low costs can be incentives, too. To learn more about home funerals visit **www.homefuneralalliance.org**

What are the emotional advantages of a home funeral?

This modern style of burial, a throwback to times before funeral homes existed, gained national exposure a few years ago when the parents of a young girl decided they could not hand their child's body over to a funeral home to be processed and stored. The mother said she'd brought her daughter into the world and she would take her through to the end. Together the mother and father bathed her, dressed her and carried her the few feet to her bedroom where family, friends and neighbors came to say goodbye. Video interviews with families who've held home funerals can be found on **www.Youtube.com**.

Bodies do not look remarkably different after death than they did at death. Many people who die after a long illness have not been eating or drinking for days and there is little or no release of fluids when they die. A home funeral guide can help mourners know what to expect.

Families find washing and dressing the body after death to be especially comforting and spiritual. Knowing no one else will so intimately touch the person who has died or see the body of their loved one without clothing can be a real comfort and give a sense of accomplishment.

Families say being able to spend flexible time with the body 24 hours a day in their home for saying goodbye offers family and friends real closure that an hour long visitation at a funeral home cannot provide. Children are reported as understanding and accepting the death more easily than at a funeral provider, and they can be put to work writing poems, painting a simple casket or adding notes to the inside of the casket before the body is removed from the house.

Some families choose to drive their loved one to the crematory or cemetery themselves – a cardboard casket will fit in many SUVs to take their loved one that "last mile." Doing so requires a permit from the county or state.

Would you consider a home funeral? Why or why not?

What are other new and upcoming methods for body disposition?

Cremation is popular overseas where there is less available land for cemeteries because the lands have been settled for hundreds or even thousands of years. At least one country leases graves for twenty years at a time; bones are moved to an ossuary (metal or stone box) if the family decides not to renew the lease.

There are a number of processes being developed and used in Europe that will eventually make their way here. One technique includes freezing the body then shaking it to eliminate all water, leaving only solid matter which is ground like cremains.

Another technique called “resomation” (which is available in several states now) uses hot water to leave only solids that can be broken up the same way crematory remains are ground. A few (very) hardy people take this solid matter and use it in their gardens as fertilizer.

An Italian company is creating eco-conscious egg-shaped “pods” bodies can be folded into then buried with a tree or other plant on top that gets all its nutrition from the pod.

A company near Chicago creates real diamonds from cremains. Their equipment uses pressure and heat over several months to simulate the environment in which diamonds are formed in nature. A 1-carat flawless diamond costs about the same as a big funeral and burial.

Japan is experimenting with multi-story "cemetery buildings."

Composting is being explored in the northwest part of the country. Proponents say it will be less expensive and will produce excellent soil in a closed system.

As the environment gets more attention and cemetery land gets difficult to find more new methods to dispose of earthly remains will be available.

Pre-Planning and Pre-paying For Your Own Funeral With A Funeral Home: A Gimmick

There are as many as three times the number of funeral homes and crematories as are needed in some areas of the country. As more people choose cremation and alternative burial methods like green burial (which require only a few services from a provider) there are fewer traditional funeral customers paying full price to all those providers. Funeral homes must make every opportunity count and pre-planning with customers is in their best interests... but it may not be in yours.

At funeral home directors' conferences the marketing push is on to sell babyboomers a big funeral at today's prices on the premise that no one else will have to be responsible for creating and paying for the funeral when it's needed (and theoretically more expensive) in the future. It sounds good but you could end up paying much more over time. Some things to think about:

1. The plans you make with a locally-owned funeral home and the payments you make to that business may, according to your contract with the provider, be

limited to use at that provider only.

2. The money you invest will no longer be yours, and you may pay high interests rates on monthly payment plans.

3. If you move out of state or change your mind about your choices the provider might refuse to pay out for services or to issue a refund so you can be buried in your new location. If you go to a different funeral home, the provider you made the plans with will not be obligated to make that money available to another facility.

4. There are too many stories of customers being told that prices have gone up and they must pay more for the same plans they made years ago for it to be just an urban legend.

5. There have been occasions, too, where the funeral home was sold and the new owner has no records of plans or funds.

6. You can also pre-pay by taking out a life insurance policy. Most funeral homes work with a insurance partner who offers insurance to you at a high interest rate, then pays the policy face value directly to the funeral home at the time of need, which can lead to higher expenses.

Either way you could pay more than you should over many years and you won't see any of the interest you might have earned had you kept the money. It will belong to the funeral provider.

Some states, like Florida, have a state-wide general trust that pre-planning funds are deposited into to hold the money rather than allowing individual funeral providers to hold it. This trust is operated by the state funeral directors association.

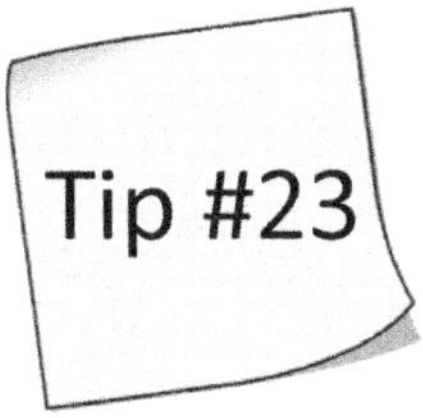

Standard pre-planning contracts use the following disclaimer: "**The Price Of These Goods And Services Is Not Guaranteed.**" What good is a locked-in price if it's not locked in?

What's the best way to put money aside for a future funeral?

Open a "Payable On Death" savings account. This special type of bank account allows you to designate the person who will be given access to the funds in the account when you die (assign it to your spouse or your adult child – you can change it later if needed). Other accounts you have in just your name may be "frozen" upon death or held up in court for months or longer but this one will free up funds immediately.

The POD account releases the funds when they have the death certificate in hand. The account pays you interest over time.

Will you end up paying more when you need a funeral so many years from now than if you pay for the full funeral now? Possibly, but your fund will grow over time, too. And it's just as likely that new and less expensive methods of disposition will be available. Importantly, you will control your money, not a funeral provider.

How do you want your body to be disposed of? Would you have your ashes put into fireworks and sent off with a bang? What would you absolutely *not* want done when you die?

Made in the USA
Monee, IL
04 November 2026

67378328R00066